What Mary Jo Shared

JANICE MAY UDRY
Pictures: Eleanor Mill

HARCOURT BRACE & COMPANY

Orlando   Atlanta   Austin   Boston   San Francisco   Chicago   Dallas   New York
Toronto   London

This edition is published by special arrangement with Albert Whitman & Company.

Grateful acknowledgment is made to Albert Whitman & Company for permission to reprint *What Mary Jo Shared* by Janice May Udry, illustrated by Eleanor Mill. Text copyright © 1966 by Janice May Udry; illustrations copyright © 1966 by Eleanor Mill. Originally published in hardcover by Albert Whitman & Company.

Printed in the United States of America

ISBN 0-15-305746-7

1 2 3 4 5 6 7 8 9 10   059   97   96   95   94

What Mary Jo Shared

Mary Jo never shared anything at school. She was too shy to stand before the other children and tell about anything. She didn't think they would listen to her.

Almost every day her teacher, Miss Willet, would say, "And Mary Jo, do you have something to share with us this morning?"

Mary Jo always shook her head and looked at the floor.

"Why don't you ever share anything?" her friend Laurie asked.

"I will some day," said Mary Jo. "I just don't want to yet."

Mary Jo really did want to share, but she was afraid to try.

Almost every evening when he came home, Mary Jo's father asked, "Did you share something at school today, Mary Jo?"

"Not yet," she always answered.

One morning it was raining hard.

"I'll share my new umbrella," thought Mary Jo as soon as she woke up and saw the rain pouring down the window. She could hardly wait. She hurried with breakfast and hurried with dressing.

Finally it was time to put on her new pink raincoat and take her own pink umbrella to school. This was the first umbrella she had ever owned. Before, when it rained, she walked under her sister's umbrella. She had picked this one out herself in the store. On the handle was a chain and tag. Mary Jo had written her name, the name of the school, and "Room 101" on the tag herself.

She hurried up the hill from the car, holding her umbrella against the heavy rain. At the door she shook her umbrella and then carried it in, dripping along the hall. When she got to the door of her room, she saw a whole row of umbrellas drying in the hall! They were all sizes and colors. Some of the other umbrellas even had tags on the handles like Mary Jo's.

"Almost everybody in my room has an umbrella, too," thought Mary Jo. "I guess that isn't a good thing to share after all."

So when Miss Willet said, "And Mary Jo, do you have something to share with us this morning?" Mary Jo shook her head and looked at the floor.

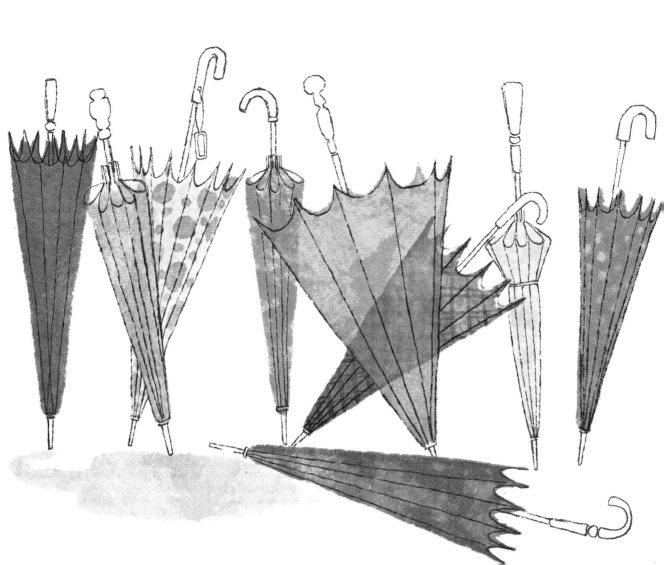

The next week Mary Jo and her brother caught a grasshopper and put it in a jar with holes punched on top so it could breathe.

"I'll share the grasshopper!" thought Mary Jo.

She wrapped the jar carefully in a cloth and put it in a paper bag. That way, even if she dropped the jar, it wouldn't break. She hurried to school carrying the wrapped jar carefully under one arm and her lunch box in the other hand.

When she came to the door of her room, several children were clustered around a boy named Jimmy. They were all looking at something he had brought in a jar.

Mary Jo put her lunch box and sack carefully on the shelf. She hung up her sweater. Then she went to see what the other children were looking at.

"Jimmy's got *six* grasshoppers in a jar!" said Laurie. "He caught all of them himself."

Mary Jo thought about her one grasshopper—and how her brother had helped her catch it.

"I guess I won't share my grasshopper after all," thought Mary Jo.

So when Miss Willet said, "And Mary Jo, do you have something to share with us this morning?" Mary Jo shook her head and looked at the floor.

All the other children in Miss Willet's room shared things. They shared letters from their aunts, or they shared their pets—turtles, white mice, rabbits, and kittens. They shared things they found at the beach and things they found in the woods.

Mary Jo didn't have an aunt to get letters from, she didn't have any pets, and she never found anything at the beach or in the woods that someone else hadn't already shared.

But Mary Jo finally became determined to share something that no one else had shared. It got so she could hardly think of anything else.

One night she even dreamed that she wanted to share her new pet elephant. But when she brought him to Miss Willet's room, he was too big to squeeze through the door, no matter how hard she shoved! So—in her dream—she sadly led her new pet away.

"What shall I share?" she pondered over and over.

Her father came home. "Did you share something at school today, Mary Jo?" he asked her as usual.

And as usual, Mary Jo said, "Not yet."

Then, suddenly, Mary Jo thought of something!

"Could you go to school with me tomorrow for a little while?" she asked her father.

"Tomorrow? Yes," said her father. "I don't have a class until eleven o'clock." Mary Jo's father was a teacher in the high school.

"Good!" said Mary Jo. "Then you can come and hear me share something!"

"All right," said her father, "I'll be there! What are you going to share?"

"Wait and see," said Mary Jo.

As soon as Mary Jo and her father got to school the next morning, Mary Jo introduced her father to Miss Willet.

Miss Willet said that they were very glad to have him visit their class.

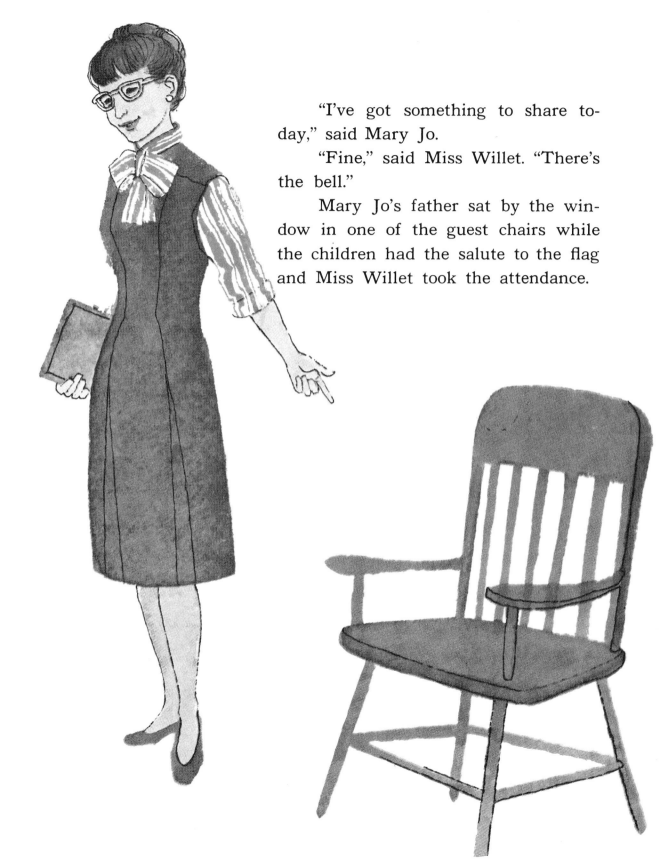

"I've got something to share to-day," said Mary Jo.

"Fine," said Miss Willet. "There's the bell."

Mary Jo's father sat by the window in one of the guest chairs while the children had the salute to the flag and Miss Willet took the attendance.

Then it was Sharing Time. As soon as Miss Willet asked if anyone had anything to share, Mary Jo raised her hand.

"Mary Jo," said Miss Willet. "You may share with us first this morning."

Mary Jo stood up and walked to the front of the room for the first time.

"This morning I have brought my *Father* to share!" she said. In spite of herself she giggled a little. This made all the children smile, and they turned to look at Mary Jo's father.

He didn't mind at all. He stood, bowed his head a little in his friendly way, and waited to be shared.

"This is my father, Mr. William Wood. He is thirty-six years old and has a wife and three children. His youngest child is me," said Mary Jo.

Jimmy raised his hand. "My father was born in Montana," said Jimmy. "Where was your father born?"

"My father was born in California," said Mary Jo. "He teaches English in high school. He likes to read a lot, and he writes quite a bit, too. He is a good swimmer and knows how to sail boats. He likes to go fishing and hiking."

"So does my father!" said Laurie.

"My father builds houses," said another child.

"My father travels all over the country," said another.

They *all* wanted to share their fathers, it seemed.

"Children," said Miss Willet, "it is Mary Jo who is sharing her father today. Please be a little more quiet."

"Before my father grew up, he was a little boy," said Mary Jo. Then her face turned hot because that sounded sort of silly.

All the children laughed. But Mary Jo went on.

"Sometimes he wasn't too well behaved," said Mary Jo.

"What did he do?" asked one of the boys.

"Well, once he locked his little brother out of the house. . . . .

. . . . And once he ate all the cake his mother was saving for an afternoon club meeting," said Mary Jo. "And now, my father will say a few words."

Mr. Wood smiled and made a little speech about how he had enjoyed visiting Miss Willet's class.

The children clapped, and Mary Jo and her father sat down.

Mary Jo felt good. At last she had shared something that no one else had thought of sharing.